The American War 1812–14

Philip Katcher · Illustrated by Bryan Fosten

Series editor Martin Windrow

First published in Great Britain in 1990 by
Osprey Publishing, Midland House, West Way,
Botley, Oxford OX2 0PH, UK
443 Park Avenue South, New York, NY 10016, USA
Email: info@ospreypublishing.com

© 1990 Osprey Publishing Ltd.
Previously published as MAA 36
Reproduced here with new artwork
Reprinted 1992, 1995, 1998, 1999, 2001, 2004, 2005

British Library Cataloguing in Publication Data
Katcher, Philip 1941–
    The American war. — (Men-at-arms series).
    1. United States. War of 1812
    I. Title   II. Series
    973.52

ISBN 0 85045 197 3

Series Editor: MARTIN WINDROW

Filmset in Great Britain
Printed in China through World Print Ltd.

FOR A CATALOGUE OF ALL BOOKS PUBLISHED BY
OSPREY MILITARY AND AVIATION PLEASE CONTACT:

NORTH AMERICA
Osprey Direct, 2427 Bond Street,
University Park, IL 60466, USA
E-mail: info@ospreydirectusa.com

ALL OTHER REGIONS
Osprey Direct UK, P.O. Box 140,
Wellingborough, Northants, NN8 2FA, UK
E-mail: info@ospreydirect.co.uk

www.ospreypublishing.com

Artist's note

Readers may care to note that the original paintings
from which the colour plates in this book were
prepared are available for private sale. All
reproduction copyright whatsoever is retained by the
Publishers. All enquiries should be addressed to:
    Bryan Fosten
    5 Ross Close
    Nyetimber
    Nr. Bognor Regis
    Sussex PO21 3JW
The Publishers regret that they can enter into no
correspondence upon this matter.

The War

Typically the United States is said to have declared war on Great Britain in 1812 because of the Royal Navy's impressment of American seamen from American ships and the British desire to create an Indian buffer state between the growing expansion of the United States and Canada. Actually, an Englishman who had lived in the United States for eight years before the war's outbreak, William Cobbett, probably described the real cause. 'There seemed to be wanting just such a war as this to complete the separation of England from America; and to make the latter feel that she had no safety against the former but in the arms of her free citizens.'

Regardless of the reasons, however, on 4 June 1812, U.S. President James Madison, asked Congress to declare war. The House of Representatives approved quickly, but the Senate agreed only after debate, on 18 June, and only by six votes. The feelings which divided the Senate were felt throughout the entire American public.

War, it was, regardless of any feelings. Although a main cause may have been maritime, it was obvious to the most jingoistic of American politicians that the small American Navy had no chance of defeating His Majesty's enormous fleets.

On the other hand, a quick victory could be won by the prompt capture of Canada, which could then be held until Great Britain gave in to American demands.

Canada's capture presented no problems to the American Army – at least in the politician's minds. Ex-President Thomas Jefferson wrote in 1812 that, 'The acquisition of Canada this year as far as the neighbourhood of Quebec will be a mere matter of marching.' Kentucky Congressman Henry Clay told Congress, 'The conquest of Canada is in your power. I trust I shall not be deemed presumptuous when I state I verily believe that the militia of Kentucky are alone competent to place Montreal and Upper Canada at your feet.' Canada, then, would be the first target and would be captured even before Great Britain, involved in a major war already, could send troops to capture any American towns.

Considering its size, Canada was garrisoned by relatively few troops. Major-General George Glasgow had 450 gunners in four companies of the Royal Artillery. The 1st/8th (King's), 41st, 49th, and 100th Regiments of Foot were in the colony, as well as the 10th Royal Veteran Battalion. The Royal Newfoundland Regiment of Fencible Infantry and other Canadian fencibles had been raised locally. The Engineer Department consisted of a lieutenant-colonel and four captains. All told, this came to some 5,600 effectives of which 1,200 were in Upper Canada.

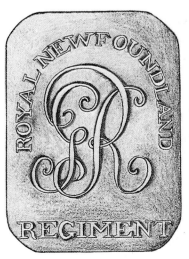

Brass belt-plate of the Royal Newfoundland Regiment of Foot. (Drawing by Rebecca Katcher)

There were few problems with the regiments. The 41st, says one authority, 'was a stout battalion of old soldiers, but unfortunate in its colonel'.

Sir Isaac Brock
(Public Archives of Canada)

Major-General Isaac Brock, Commanding Officer and Civil Governor of Upper Canada, wrote about the 49th, 'although the regiment has been ten years in this country, drinking rum without bounds, it is still respectable, and apparently ardent for an opportunity to acquire distinction.' The 100th, which had been raised in 1805 as the Prince Regent's County of Dublin Regiment, according to one authority, 'was made up of fine young Protestant Irishmen, not ill-disciplined, but a little wild.'

In Nova Scotia, not a part of Upper or Lower Canada, Sir John Sherbrooke had 161 officers and 4,220 other ranks, including 560 Royal Artillerymen and 119 Royal Military Artificers. His infantry regiments were the 2nd/8th, the 98th, less 300 men in Bermuda, and the 99th. The 104th Foot was in New Brunswick, and the Nova Scotia Fencibles was in Newfoundland.

The Americans divided their forces into the Army of the West, under Brigadier-General William Hull, which would launch its attack from Fort Detroit; the Army of the Centre, under militia General Stephen Van Rensselaer, launching its attack from Niagara, and the Army of the North, under General Henry Dearborn, which would move from Lake Champlain. While an attack from the New York–New England areas would bring greater strategic results, the war's unpopularity and lack of support in those areas led to the main attacks being delivered from the west, where the war was more favoured.

The first move was Hull's. He arrived at Detroit on 5 July 1812, with 300 men of the 1st Infantry, and the 1st, 2nd, and 3rd Ohio Militia Regiments. The 1st Infantry Regiment of Michigan Militia joined him there. Leaving the Michigan regiment and men from the 1st and 2nd Ohio, Hull moved across the river, taking the town of Sandwich. There he issued a bombastic proclamation to the people of Canada, asking them to join his army. Some 500 Canadian militiamen actually placed themselves under Hull's protection, while the Norfolk County Militia, either overawed by the proclamation or disloyal, refused to march against him.

Hull was to move north. South of him, however, was Fort Malden, garrisoned by several companies of the 41st Foot. Colonel Lewis Cass took a force made up of a Regular ranger company, five companies of Ohio infantry and a detachment of Ohio rangers, and moved south. Privates Hancock and Dean, 41st Foot, serving as pickets, were the first to see the Americans, and fired at them. An overwhelming volley answered them, leaving them both badly wounded. Hancock's was the war's first death, while Dean was taken prisoner and recovered.

The 4th Infantry reinforced Cass's troops, and the move to Malden continued. When they got there, however, the fort looked too strong to storm and they retired to Sandwich.

Meanwhile, further north, Captain Charles Roberts, 10th Royal Veteran Battalion, received word war had been declared. Gathering some 180–230 of his own men and local militia and 400 Indians, he set off for the American Fort Michilimackinac. That fort was garrisoned by sixty-one men commanded by artillery officer Lieutenant Porter Hanks, who had not been warned of the war. Roberts placed a six-pounder gun on the heights commanding the fort, and, seeing resistance was impossible, Hanks surrendered.

The loss of this fort to his north, and Fort Malden standing to his south badly shook Hull's already shaky morale. He withdrew across the river to the wooden stockade of Fort Detroit on 5 August.

With that, Brock, now commanding Fort Malden, was ready to take the initiative. His troops now numbered nine officers and 270 other ranks of the 41st Foot; one officer of Royal Engineers; one officer and twenty-five other ranks of the Royal Artillery, and one officer and seventy other ranks of the Royal Newfoundland Regiment. By 15 August Brock had five guns in position opposing Fort Detroit, and began firing. The next morning he took his Regulars and militia, and dressed the latter in old 41st coatees, mixing them one militiaman to every two Regulars to give the impression of a large regular force. Besides them, he had 1,000 Indians under Tecumseh, the most important Indian leader of the time.

Before he could launch the grand attack, Hull, fearful of letting the Indians loose among the fort's civilians, surrendered. Brock had captured the 4th Infantry, detachments from the 1st and 3rd Infantry, two squadrons of cavalry, one company of artillery, the 1st, 2nd and 3rd Ohio and the 1st Michigan. Another of his prizes was a cannon with markings indicating it had been originally captured by the Americans at the Battle of Saratoga, 17 October 1777.

The day after the surrender, the Americans abandoned Fort Dearborn, were ambushed on the march and massacred by Indians. The Army of the West was no more.

Brock, however, was not going to sit back with two more American armies threatening Canada. Immediately, he transferred most of his troops to face Van Rensselaer's army.

Van Rensselaer was a New York militia general with no active military experience. He, his 900 Regulars and 3,000 militiamen were at Lewiston, while Regular Brigadier-General Alexander Smyth, his 1,650 Regulars and 400 militiamen were at Buffalo. Some 1,300 Regulars were also at Fort Niagara.

Van Rensselaer had command of the entire army, due to a problem in American Army Regulations. The senior officer, be he militia or Regular, was always in command – regardless of ability or experience. In the British Army command went to the Regular, even if he had to be given temporary, local rank. According to British Army Regulations no militia officer of about equal rank to a Regular would ever command him. That this was not true in the American Army was a fatal flaw.

As it turned out, Smyth would not assist nor even hardly speak to Van Rensselaer. The reverse was equally true. Still, Van Rensselaer was willing and eager to attack, which was not the case with Smyth, and therefore planned a move by his own troops.

He planned to move across the Niagara River, capturing Queenston and its heights. From this area he would command the entire river and drive the British out of the Niagara Peninsula. On 13 October he began his attack. In the first assault wave were some 300 men of the 13th Infantry and an equal number of New York militiamen. Quickly they made it up the winding footpath to the heights overlooking Queenston. A detachment of the 49th held a redan there, but the Americans came on with the bayonet and drove them out.

Out of the ten Regular officers in the force, two were killed and five seriously wounded, and Captain John Wool, 13th Infantry, took command. Brock, in the town, quickly reassembled his forces, and personally led a counter-attack back to the redan. In the heavy American fire Brock fell mortally wounded while urging his men on. The counter-attack was driven off.

Wool had also fallen badly wounded, and was taken off to the American shore. But reinforcements were arriving, the first among them being men of the 6th Infantry. Most of the New York militiamen, however, were less than eager to get into the fray, and refused to get into the boats. It was the law, they pointed out, that militia need not serve outside the borders of their own state. While these legal questions were being debated on the American shore, Lieutenant-Colonel Winfield Scott, 2nd Artillery, had taken command of the troops on the heights.

Although Brock was dead the British were far from giving up. Reinforcements for their side

The Battle of Queenston Heights, drawn by an eyewitness. (Public Archives of Canada)

Uniform worn by General Brock at Queenston Heights. The small hole in the centre of the coat, about level with the fourth button down, is the fatal bullet hole. (National Museums of Canada)

Infantry; Captain Towson's Artillery; the Fourteenth and Twentythird Infantry as one regiment; Captain Barker's and Captain Branch's Artillery; the Twelfth and Twentieth Infantry; Captain Archer's Artillery; General Tannehill's (Pennsylvania Volunteer) Infantry; a company of riflemen; General Porter's (New York Volunteer Infantry; a battalion of Riflemen on each flank, in a line perpendicular to that formed by the main army, extending to the front and rear.' Despite these fine plans, Smyth seemed unable to get organized enough actually to get all the men across the river. The militia simply went home. Finally, at the end of November, the Regulars went into winter quarters, and three months later Smyth's name was quietly dropped from the army rolls.

While all this marching about was going on Dearborn had moved his seven Regular regiments, with artillery and dragoons, to Plattsburg. There he announced he would lead his army to Montreal but Canadian militia and Indians drove his advance guard back at the village of Champlain. His New York and Vermont militia thereupon refused to march further, and all hopes for a quick capture of Canada in 1812 were finished.

Brass belt-plate of the 104th Regiment of Foot. (Drawing by Rebecca Katcher)

were arriving and now Major-General Roger Sheaffe, Brock's successor, sent a flank attack round the Americans' left. It was made up of men of the 41st Foot, flank companies of the 1st and 4th Lincoln Militia, three companies of the 5th Lincoln Militia, Major Merritt's Yeomanry Corps, and some militia artillery.

Tired, lacking reinforcements, having been under heavy fire all day, Colonel Scott himself wounded, the Americans surrendered.

Van Rensselaer resigned. Now Smyth, who had planned to cross the river on the other side of the famous falls, issued his orders for the invasion of Canada. The American Army was to get into boats, row across and fall out on the Canadian side, 'Beginning on the right, as follows: Captain Gibson's Artillery, the Sixth and Thirteenth

It was obvious that the Americans would continue their attempts to capture Canada in 1813, and therefore in February the 104th Foot left New Brunswick for Quebec, a total of 350 miles.

It was an unusually cold winter, and each company travelled five days apart, having to break a fresh trail through the deep snows. Officers carried their own kits in their knapsacks, while toboggans were used for provisions. Each daybreak the march would begin, ending at noon while there was still enough daylight to build a new camp. Once a blizzard forced the lead companies back to the previous day's camp, and an officer and two privates volunteered to go fifty-four miles to St André for food, which was running out. They got there and returned with the food in two days.

The whole regiment reached Quebec in twenty-four days, then went on ten more miles to Kingston. Only twenty men died from conditions aggravated by the march.

In addition, the government in London advised Canada's Governor-General, Sir George Prevost, that it was sending reinforcements consisting of the 19th Regiment of Light Dragoons, a company of Royal Artillery, detachments from the Corps of Royal Artillery Drivers and the Corps of Royal Sappers and Miners, and battalions of the 13th, 41st, 70th, 89th, 98th, 101st and 103rd Regiments of Foot and Regiments De Watteville and De Meuron.

These were good regiments, although the commander of the 70th had to report to Prevost that, 'we are very young and very small', with his best men left on recruiting duty or on furlough, and the regiment was, at best, in 'a very infant state'. The 103rd was another problem with Prevost

Contemporary print of Sir George Prevost. (McCord Museum)

complaining that it was made up of 'about 750 very young Soldiers and Boys'. Furthermore, many 103rd men turned out to be convicts taken from the hulks and almost ninety men deserted to the Americans shortly after arrival. Even 'the repeated infliction of capital punishment' did not stop the flow of deserters.

The Americans planned to return to the offensive by recapturing Detroit and attacking across Lake Ontario. Command of the new Army of the Northwest, which would do all this, was given to a military hero, Brigadier-General William H. Harrison. His army was made up of the 17th, 19th and 24th Infantry Regiments, recently recruited in the western states, and volunteers from Virginia, Pennsylvania, Kentucky and Ohio. Harrison was told to avoid using militia as much as possible and fill up the Regular regiments first.

Although winter campaigns were difficult, and the winter in that part of the world rather harsh, public opinion demanded some victories to make up for the disasters of 1812, and Harrison started towards Lake Erie in October.

In January 1813 Harrison sent on the 1st and 5th Kentucky Militia Regiments, the Kentucky Rifle Regiment and the 17th Infantry, under Brigadier-General James Winchester, to French-town, a small Canadian post on the Raisin River. There they were soundly defeated by a larger force of British, Canadians and Indians under Colonel Henry Proctor. Over 100 Kentucky riflemen were killed in action, while the Indians massacred the rest. 'Remember the Raisin!' became an American battle-cry.

That disaster caused Harrison to abandon any winter offensive plans, and he went into winter quarters to rebuild his force.

Early in spring Dearborn was ordered to capture Kingston, which was the only possible site for a naval station on the Canadian side of Lake Ontario. Its capture would give the Americans control of the lake, and cut British lines of communications between east and west. Dearborn, however, heard that the Kingston garrison had been reinforced, and switched his objective to Upper Canada's capital, York.

York was garrisoned by the grenadier and a battalion company of the 8th Foot, a company-sized detachment of the Royal Newfoundland Regiment, a company of the Glengarry Light Infantry Fencibles, the 3rd York Militia Regiment, 300 dockyard workers and 50–100 Mississauga and Chippewa Indians. Dearborn, in poor health, gave command of the invasion force to Brigadier-General Zebulon Pike, a Regular.

Pike landed his troops, consisting of Regular riflemen under Major Benjamin Forsyth, the 6th, 15th, 16th and 21st Infantry, detachments of light and heavy artillery and some .volunteers, about four miles west of the town. The landing was unopposed. The British drew up their troops in a fortification half-way between the town and the landing site.

Tin shako-plate of the 15th Infantry, the typical early .infantry design. (Drawing by Rebecca Katcher)

Resistance from the British was stiff, but Pike refused to allow his Regulars to load, sending them forward by platoons by sections to take the works at bayonet point. A howitzer of the 3rd Artillery Regiment was sent forward with the column, and the British were overwhelmed.

As the Americans pushed on and the British fled, a British powder magazine in the city blew up. General Pike was talking to a just-captured sergeant when heavy rocks, hurled about by the explosion, fell among them, killing both the General and the Sergeant. Command of the troops fell to Colonel Cromwell Pearce, 16th Infantry.

Pearce seemed unable to control his troops, who now went on the rampage, looting and burning the public buildings and records. After staying in the fire-blackened town for about a week, they left to join the troops who were to attack the forts on the Canadian side of the Niagara River.

While the Americans were busy, Sir George Prevost had gathered a force at Kingston to take Sackett's Harbor, the main American post on the lake. His force consisted of the grenadier company of the 100th Foot, a detachment from the 1st (Royal Scots) Foot, two companies of the 8th Foot, four companies of the 104th Foot, one company of Glengarry Light Infantrymen, and two companies of Canadian voltigeurs. Two six-pounder guns were included in the force.

New York militia Brigadier-General Jacob Brown commanded the garrison at Sackett's Harbor – and a motley garrison it was. He had the 1st and 2nd Regiments of Dragoons, about 250 men; some 50–60 Regular artillerymen; some 80–100 Regular infantrymen left as invalids from various regiments; new recruits for Regular regiments, and some 250 men of the Albany Volunteers.

On the night of 26 May, Prevost launched his attack. Brown divided his men into two lines: the first offered stiff resistance but was pushed aside. The second line, in already prepared fortifications, held against one, then two frontal attacks. While re-forming for yet a third attack, the British right flank was suddenly hit by the rallied American militia. That was too much. Wrote Sergeant James Commins, 8th Foot: 'We brought all our wounded away it was possible to remove and embarked on board ship tired, hungry, wet and thirsty, highly mystified, and looking very sheepish at one another; you would hardly have heard a whisper until that powerful stimulant grog was served out when the Tower of Babel was nothing like it, everyone blaming each other, nay some of them were rash and impudent to lay the blame on anyone but themselves. As for my part, I thought much but said little having got a wound in my thigh which began to pain me as soon as I got cold. . . .'

British losses had been 47 killed, 154 wounded and 16 missing. The Americans lost 21 dead and 85 wounded.

The day Prevost was moving towards Sackett's Harbor, Dearborn began invading Canada. His first move was on Fort George, on the Niagara, garrisoned by the 49th Foot, as well as detachments of the 8th, 41st, Glengarry and Royal Newfoundland Regiments. On 27 May the Americans sent the 2nd Artillery, acting as infantrymen, Forsyth's riflemen and detachments from various infantry regiments against the fort. Flanked by Maryland and New York volunteers, the British, who had advanced to stop the Americans from landing, were driven back.

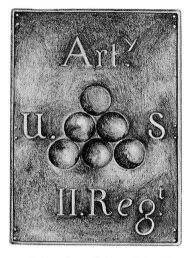

Stamped brass shako-plate of the 2nd Artillery Regiment. Other regiments used different designs, with cannon, flags and eagles. (Drawing by Rebecca Katcher)

Opposed largely by the 8th Foot, the 6th Infantry drove forward and, as American victory seemed assured, the British spiked their guns and retreated.

Upon the fort's capture, the Americans sent the 13th and 14th Infantry, with a company of the 2nd Artillery, after the retreating British. They halted at Stony Creek and were reinforced. A reconnaissance of the American position by the 8th and 49th Foot light companies showed them to be poorly arranged, and a night attack was planned.

Five companies of the 8th and the whole 49th accordingly struck at two in the morning, immediately capturing all the American artillery. The 8th smashed into the 5th, 16th and 23rd Infantry. They, supported by the 25th Infantry, at first made a stand. British troops broke through the American lines, wheeled and fired on the

Americans' backs. The Americans broke and fled.

The 2nd Dragoons charged through the 49th Foot, running into their own side, the 16th Infantry, which opened fire on them. In total confusion, the Americans fell back to Fort George. On the way they abandoned Fort Erie, which had been captured by the 12th Infantry.

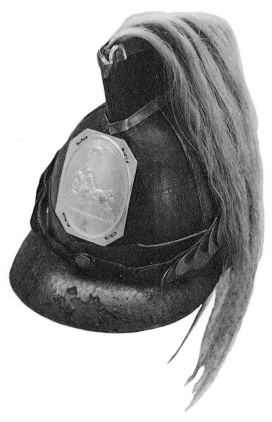

U.S. dragoon's helmet of black leather with a pewter front plate. (Fort McHenry National Monument and Historic Shrine)

Another advance party of some 500 men was ambushed and surrendered to a force of 250 British and Indians while only fifteen miles from the Fort. After these disasters there was no further northern advance made by Dearborn, who resigned in early July.

On Lake Erie itself the British fleet had been defeated and, with the Americans in control of the lake, Harrison began to move his army forward to retake Detroit. Proctor, greatly outnumbered, abandoned both Fort Malden and Detroit and

began an eastward retreat. The Indians feared being abandoned to the Americans, and pleaded for Proctor to make a stand.

Proctor picked a line on the banks of the Thames River, some eighty-five miles from Malden to make his stand. He drew up his lines with the 41st Foot in the main line, Indians on the flank. Harrison had some 120 Regulars of the 27th Infantry, and five brigades of Kentucky volunteers under the State Governor, as well as a regiment of mounted Kentucky riflemen.

Harrison, seeing the British arrangements, decided on an unusual change from the day's typical tactics. He hurled the mounted Kentuckians at the 41st. Tired, worn from long marches, the 41st fired one then two scattered volleys, and broke as the men and horses came smashing through. The British reserve line gave way just as quickly and the horsemen wheeled left and right, firing into the scattering lines.

At the same time, the infantry charged the Indians, who fought almost an hour after the last red-coated Regular fled the field. Tecumseh fell dead and the fight was over. Lake Erie was an American lake.

The main action now was the expedition against Montreal. Gathered for this drive were the 5th, 12th and 13th Infantry under General Boyd; the 6th, 15th and 22nd Infantry under General Brown; the 9th, 16th and 25th Infantry under General Covington, and the 11th, 14th and 21st Infantry under General Swartout. General Porter commanded light troops and artillery, as another brigade.

The invasion was to be a two-pronged affair with rich southerner Brigadier-General Wade Hampton moving from Plattsburg, and the other prong under Major-General James Wilkinson moving from Sackett's Harbor. As with Smyth and Van Rensselaer, the two were not even on speaking terms, which certainly did not bode any good for American arms.

Nor were the troops, even the Regulars, under their commands, all that good. Colonel Roger Purdy, 4th Infantry, wrote of Hampton's force that it was, '. . . consisting of about 4,000 men, [and] was composed principally of recruits who had been but a short time in the service, and had not been exercised with that rigid discipline so

**Lieutenant-Colonel Charles de Salaberry, commander of
the Canadian Voltigeurs. (Public Archives of Canada)**

essentially necessary to constitute the soldier. They had indeed been taught various evolutions, but a spirit of subordination was foreign to their views.'

Hampton moved his force up to the Châteaugay River, where a force of 50 Canadian fencibles, 150 Canadian voltigeurs, 100 sedentary militia and a few Indians were gathered under Lieutenant-Colonel Charles de Salaberry as a first line of defence. In reserve were 300 Canadian voltigeurs, 480 of the 2nd Battalion of Select Embodied Militia, some 150 Indians and 200 sendentary militia.

Purdy was sent with the light infantry companies of the 5th, 12th and 13th Infantry, to flank de Salaberry and attack his rear. This command ended up lost in the dense forests, and wandered about pointlessly during the entire battle.

The main American force moved forward in an equally dense forest. The resulting action when they finally came in contact with the Canadians was so confused that American units ended up firing on each other. De Salaberry had buglers give calls on the American flanks, causing them to think the force in front of them was much larger than it actually was.

When the Americans finally retreated to sort things out, fifty of their ranks had been injured, while only five Canadians were killed, sixteen wounded and four missing. Hampton fell back all the way to Plattsburg and joined the increasing ranks of resigned American general officers.

Wilkinson moved forward for his turn. He was met at Chrystler's Farm on 11 November 1813 by three companies of Canadian voltigeurs, thirty Indians, and the 89th and 49th Regiments of Foot. The 49th, normally nicknamed the 'Invincibles', were called the 'Green Tigers' by the American militia because of their green facings. Wilkinson's own force included fourteen Regular infantry regiments, a company of the 1st Rifle Regiment and two regiments, as well as three artillery regiments. The resulting action, fought in a rough clearing, intersected with small gullies and fences, was one of the war's few European-style battles.

The Americans, seeing the 49th in their grey overcoats, thought them to be militia and immediately charged, with the 21st Infantry in the lead. They quickly cleared out the Canadian skirmish line, only to be met with a crushing fire. They fell back to the shelter of the woods. The Americans then swung on to the British right, but the British Regulars crossed in front of the field in echelon, driving the Americans back by platoon volleys.

The 2nd Dragoons was then hurled at the 89th Foot but repelled. Lieutenant-Colonel Morrison, 49th Foot, wrote: 'The 49th was then directed to charge their guns posted opposite to ours, but it became necessary when within a short distance of them to check the forward movement, in consequence of a charge from their Cavalry on the right lest they should wheel about and fall upon their rear, but they were received in so gallant a manner by the Companies of the 89th under Captain Barnes and the well directed fire of the Artillery, that they quickly retreated and by an immediate charge from those Companies one Gun was gained. The Enemy immediately concentrated their Force to check our advance but such was the steady countenance and well directed fire of our Troops and Artillery that about half past four they gave way at all points from an exceeding strong position endeavouring by their Light Infty. to cover their retreat, who were soon driven away by a judicious movement made by Lt. Col. Pearson.' The 21st Infantry, under Lieutenant-Colonel Timothy Upham, held the British back as the Americans made their retreat.

The British loss was 22 killed, 148 wounded and 9 missing. The Americans lost 102 killed, 237 wounded and 100 missing. Wilkinson's invasion of Canada was over.

While all of this was going on the British quietly retook Fort George and the Americans Fort Niagara. The Americans previously had burned the town of Newark and part of Queenston and the British retaliated by burning Buffalo and Black Rock.

In 1813 a new theatre of war had opened. A force of Regulars under General Wilkinson, who had not yet gone north, moved into a long-disputed area of west Florida and met no opposition from the Spanish. Shortly thereafter, however, the Creek Indians, inspired by Tecumseh's successes, took to the war-path in Alabama, beginning with a massacre of 500 men, women and children at Fort Mims.

Tennessee State Militia General Andrew

Jackson quickly assembled an army of Tennessee militia and moved into Indian territory. He was forced to wait at Fort Strother until, in February 1814, the 39th Infantry arrived as reinforcements.

Contemporary glass painting of Andrew Jackson. (Smithsonian Institution)

With these fresh Regulars, Jackson moved out at the end of the month to attack the Indian fortified town at the Horseshoe Bend of the Tallapoosa River. With the 39th as the main storming party, supported by the East Tennessee Brigade, the troops stormed through the Indians' fortifications and routed them. All but 100 of the braves were killed. Jackson won an appointment as a Regular major-general.

In the same year Admiral Sir George Cockburn was sent to the Chesapeake Bay area to make a diversion in favour of the northern defenders of Canada. After a failure to take the naval yard at Norfolk, which had been defended by some 580 Regulars and militia and 150 sailors and marines, Cockburn moved towards Hampton, Virginia. The local militia of some 450 was quickly overwhelmed, and the town looted and burned.

'Well!' wrote Colonel Napier, 102nd Foot, 'whatever horrible acts were done at Hampton,

they were not done by the Hundred and Second, for they were never let to quit their ranks, and they almost mutinied at my preventing them joining in the sack of the unfortunate town. The marine artillery behaved like soldiers; they had it in their power to join in the sack and refused.' The main culprits were the Chasseurs Britannique, a unit recruited from among French prisoners of war. It had just returned from a punishment tour at Botany Bay, Australia, and, according to Napier, were 'the greatest rascals existing'. Furthermore, 'Much I wished to shoot some, but had no opportunity. They really murdered without object but the pleasure of murdering.' After this episode, the unit's services were dispensed with.

Napier's own 102nd had some men from New South Wales, too, and were known as the 'Botany Bay Rangers'. Their discipline was obviously above reproach, however.

The year 1813 had not proved totally successful for anyone, but less for the Americans than for Canada's defenders. In March 1814 Wilkinson sent Regular Brigadier-General Brown to attempt to take Kingston from Plattsburg. He was given the 9th, 11th, 21st, 15th Infantry and the 3rd Artillery and a company of the 2nd Artillery. This force was met and turned back by only some 200 British and Canadian troops – another total failure.

Brown had showed his worth in previous actions, however, and was then named to command the entire Niagara–Lake Ontario theatre. Major-General George Izard was given command of the theatre from Lake Champlain to the frontier. Good officers were finally being found in the American ranks.

Brown's troops consisted of Brigadier-General Winfield Scott's brigade of the 9th, 11th, 22nd and 25th Infantry Regiments; Brigadier-General Eleazer Ripley's brigade of the 21st, 23rd and 29th Infantry Regiments, 327 regular artillerymen, 600 Pennsylvania Volunteers and 600 Indians.

Brown was ordered to cross the Niagara River around Fort Erie, take the fort and then move against Fort George or take a bridge over the Chippewa River.

On 3 July Scott crossed the river below Fort Erie with the 9th, 11th, parts of the 22nd and 25th Infantry and some artillery. Ripley, with the

19th, 21st and 23rd Infantry, followed that night. The 100th Foot sent forward men to fight a delaying action, while the 19th Light Dragoons charged into the 9th Infantry which drove them away easily. The Americans had their foothold.

On 4 July Scott, joined by some 500 Pennsylvania Volunteers and 400 Indians, moved forward to Chippewa. During the night the British defenders were joined by the 1st and 8th Foot, a detachment of Royal Artillery, the 2nd Regiment of Lincoln militia and some Indians. Scott arranged his troops with the 9th and part of the 21st on the right, the 11th in the centre and the 25th on the left. The British, under General Riall, had a van of light companies, then the 100th and the 2nd Lincoln militia, with 300 Indians on the right.

The Americans came forward, under heavy fire, to within some eighty paces of the British line, then wavered, stopping to return the British volleys. Scott, in the romantic tradition of the period, is said to have called out to the 11th Infantry, 'The enemy says we are good at the long shot, but can not stand the cold iron! I call upon the 11th instantly to give lie to that slander! Charge!'

Whatever the actual command was, charge they did, along with the 22nd. The 25th was ordered to advance arms, actually a form of shouldering arms where the musket is carried in the hand of the right arm with the muzzle pointing straight in the air. Cool as if on a parade ground, they did so and joined in the general advance. The British line crumbled and broke.

The Americans lost 61 killed, 255 wounded and 19 missing, while the British losses to the more accurate and rapid American fire were 236 killed, 322 wounded and 46 missing. The action had been especially heavy on the British Regulars, with Prevost being informed that, 'The Royals (1st Foot) & 100th Regt. are in the greatest want for Officers – The latter has but one Captain & 3 Subalterns doing duty, and about 250 effective men.'

Reinforcements were rushed forward. Brown, faced with being overwhelmed by the British, withdrew from Queenston. He sent Scott to draw out the British along the Queenston Road. Scott ran into the troops from the Chippewa and the Glengarry Light Infantry Fencibles, the 84th and 104th Foot, detachments of the Royal Artillery and some incorporated and sedentary militia at Lundy's Lane.

Both brass and pewter belt-plates of the Glengarry Light Infantry are known. (Drawing by Rebecca Katcher)

Scott came forward with the 9th, 11th and 20th Infantry, while sending the 25th along the Queenston Road. The American charge was beaten back. The key to the field seemed to be a hill held by a battery of Royal Artillery, and the 1st Infantry was ordered to draw enemy fire, while the 21st was ordered by Brown to 'storm that work and take it.' 'I'll try, sir,' was 21st commander Lieutenant-Colonel James Miller's reply.

Try he did, and the hill with seven guns fell to American bayonets. Wrote the senior British General on the field, General Drummond, 'Of so determined a Character were the attacks directed against our Guns that our Artillery Men were bayonetted by the Enemy in the Act of loading, and the muzzles of the Enemy's Guns were advanced to within a few Yards of ours.'

Quickly reinforced by the 1st and 23rd Infantry, Miller's troops stood off two equally determined British counter-attacks. The battle was the hardest fought of the war. The 11th Infantry lost its commander, every company commander was dead or wounded and, out of ammunition, finally retired from the field. The 22nd, badly battered, formed with the equally battered 9th Infantry to form one unit.

The battle itself see-sawed until about midnight when an exhausted American army withdrew. An equally exhausted British army held the field, unable to follow. Both General Phineas Riall and Drummond were wounded, and Riall was taken prisoner. On the other side, both Brown and Scott were severely wounded and Scott saw no more service that war.

The Americans lost 171 killed, 572 wounded and 110 missing, while the British lost 84 killed, 559 wounded and 193 missing. The 84th alone took 254 casualties, and the Incorporated Militia Battalion of Upper Canada, 142.

The Americans withdrew to Fort Erie, which they garrisoned with the 9th, 11th, 19th, 21st and 23rd Infantry, detachments from the 1st and 4th Rifle Regiments and New York and Pennsylvania Volunteers. Receiving further reinforcements at the beginning of August, the British set siege to the fort, but a successful sally forced them to halt the siege on 21 September. On 5 November, the Americans destroyed the fort and withdrew to American soil.

Brass shako-plate of the 1st Rifle Regiment. (Drawing by Rebecca Katcher)

With the fall of Napoleon, the British were finally able to send hardened combat veterans to Canada to finish off the Americans. On 1 September 1814 Lieutenant-General Sir John Sherbrooke was able to take the 1st company of Royal

Wings worn by Captain Benjamin Burch, District of Columbia artillery militia. (Smithsonian Institution)

Artillery, two companies of the 7th/60th Foot, and detachments of the 29th, 62nd and 98th Foot to land at Castine, in Maine. The small, rapidly gathered militia force was quickly brushed aside and Maine, which had really not been in favour of the war, surrendered. Earlier Moose Island, Maine, had fallen to the 102nd Foot.

Then, on 19 August, Major-General Robert Ross landed near Washington with the 4th, 21st, 44th and 85th Foot, some Royal Marines and sailors. He began his march to Washington, only to be met at Bladensburg by a hastily gathered force including detachments of the 12th, 36th and 38th Infantry, a squadron of Regular dragoons, two companies of light artillery, two rifle companies and an odd assortment of Maryland and Virginia militia. In a short fight, the British Regulars easily pushed through the Americans and captured their capital city. The public buildings, except the patent office and one newspaper office, were burned in retaliation for the burning of York. After a few days they re-embarked and moved north to capture Baltimore, Maryland.

Maryland militia General Samuel Smith drew up his troops to meet them at North Point. The front line was made up of the 5th Maryland on the right, some artillery, and then the 27th Maryland. The 39th and 51st Maryland Regiments formed a second line, with the 6th Maryland in reserve.

Ross sent forward the light companies of his regiments with some marines. Among the latter was a corps of colonial marines, formed by Cochrane from escaped slaves earlier that year. The corps had been united with three companies of the 2nd Battalion of Royal Marines to form a 3rd Battalion, and their record had been excellent in the various raids along the coast.

The 44th was then sent in on the front, with the 4th Foot sent around the American flank. The 39th Maryland was ordered to meet that move, with the 51st Maryland sent to fill out the flank line. For some reason the 51st broke and ran, closely followed by the 39th. The 27th Maryland held, and allowed the rest of the troops to make a fairly orderly withdrawal. Ross was killed, and the next day his replacement, Colonel Arthur Brooke, 44th Foot, moved the army up to where a well-fortified, overwhelming militia force was

The beaver shako worn by Ensign John Reese, 5th Maryland Infantry Regiment, at the Battle of North Point. (Fort McHenry National Monument and Historic Shrine)

waiting. The naval attack on Fort McHenry, made that evening, failed, and the British withdrew.

Two days before the failure of the Baltimore attack, a much more serious threat was beaten off by the Americans.

A major force had left Plattsburg for the Niagara frontier, leaving Brigadier-General Alexander Macomb with nothing more for his garrison than a company of light artillery, the 13th Infantry, a company of the 15th Infantry, detachments of the 6th, 29th, 30th, 33rd and 34th Infantry, two artillery companies, 803 sick and invalided men and 200 infantrymen serving as marines on the American fleet in Lake Champlain.

Prevost saw his chance to deliver a telling blow against the Americans and moved towards Plattsburg with Major-General Robinson's brigade of the 3rd/27th, 39, 76th and 88th Foot, Major-General Brisbane's brigade of the 2nd/8th, 13th and 49th Foot, de Meuron's Regiment, the Canadian voltigeurs and Canadian chasseurs, and Major-General Power's brigade of the 3rd, 5th, 1st/27th and 58th Foot. Each brigade was supported with an artillery brigade of five six-pounders, two twenty-four-pounders and one 5·5-inch howitzer. The 19th Light Dragoons

The national colour of the 13th Infantry Regiment. (West Point Collections, United States Military Academy)

was also a part of the expedition.

On 6 September he arrived at Plattsburg, having been only slightly slowed down by delaying actions of the 13th Infantry. There he waited a week for his naval support to begin its attack.

On 11 September that support was at hand, and he ordered a joint attack. He sent forward the light infantry companies, the 3rd/27th and 76th Foot and Power's brigade, which pushed aside the Clinton and Essex Militia and was ready to fall on the American Regulars when word arrived of the naval defeat. Without British control of Lake Champlain Plattsburg was too difficult to supply, and Prevost, much to the disgust of his veterans of the Peninsular campaign, withdrew.

News of the British failures at Baltimore and Plattsburg reached the diplomats discussing peace terms in Belgium, but the British had one more card to play. Major-General Sir Edward Pakenham, brother-in-law to the Duke of Wellington, was sent to command the 4th, 21st, 44th, 85th, 93rd and 95th Foot, the 1st and 5th West India Regiments and the 14th Light Dragoons in an attempt to capture New Orleans and remove Louisiana from the United States. The army was soon joined by the 7th (Royal Fusiliers), 40th and 43rd Foot, more élite, veteran regiments.

The first plan was to take the city by taking Mobile, guarded by some 130 men of the 2nd Infantry at Fort Bowyer, and coming down on it from the north. The 2nd stood firm, driving the

British off, and the only way left was to come up the river from the south.

Defending was Andrew Jackson with a mixed lot of militia and the 7th and 44th Infantry. Undermining British morale in a night attack, Jackson withdrew to a line of fortifications along the river, with his flanks resting in swamps. There he placed Indians, then some Tennessee and Kentucky militia, his Tennessee Rifles, the 44th Infantry, two free Negro battalions, the New Orleans Volunteer Battalion the 7th Infantry and the New Orleans Sharpshooters. Some Kentucky militia guarded the other side of the bank. Besides these men he had seven artillery batteries, including one composed of local pirates.

Detail of the coat worn by Andrew Jackson at the Battle of New Orleans. (Smithsonian Institution)

After the failure of an artillery duel, Pakenham decided on a frontal attack, with the 95th Foot sent to take the other side of the river. On the morning of 8 January his army, led by the 44th Foot, appeared in front of the American works and started across the muddy ground towards them.

The Americans fired in four ranks, each rank firing, falling back, reloading and then advancing, so a perfect stream of fire was kept up. One British officer wrote that his men fell 'like blades of grass beneath the scythe'. Another said that, 'Never before had British veterans quailed, but there was something in that leaden torrent no man on earth could face. In minutes the entire column was broken and disorganized.'

Major Thomas Wilkinson, 21st Foot, reached the American parapets alone, hit twelve times. There he fell, and an American officer told him, 'Bear up, Major. You're too brave to die.'

Wilkinson replied, 'I thank you with all my heart, but do me a favour. Tell my commander I died here on your parapet.' His body, covered with Kentucky militia colours, was carried to the rear.

On the flank the 95th Foot did better, breaking through the militia, but the main effort was a total failure. Pakenham was killed, dying in the arms of the same officer who caught Ross not too many months before.

For ten days the shattered remnant of the British Army remained there, undisturbed. Then they left. In a last-ditch effort they returned to Mobile, this time capturing Fort Bowyer. Before they could move on the city itself, word arrived that, on Christmas Eve, a treaty of peace had been signed.

If the war proved anything – none of the points which made the Americans declare war were even mentioned in the peace treaty – it was that America could not successfully invade and hold Canada, nor could the British successfully invade and hold America. That lesson, at least, seems to have been learned.

The British Army

At the war's outbreak the British Army was at the height of its glory. Wellington, the 'Iron Duke', with an army of red-coated heroes was vanquishing Napoleon's marshals one after another on the Iberian Peninsula. For almost a generation the army had been tempered in war against the French; it was tough, well trained, and

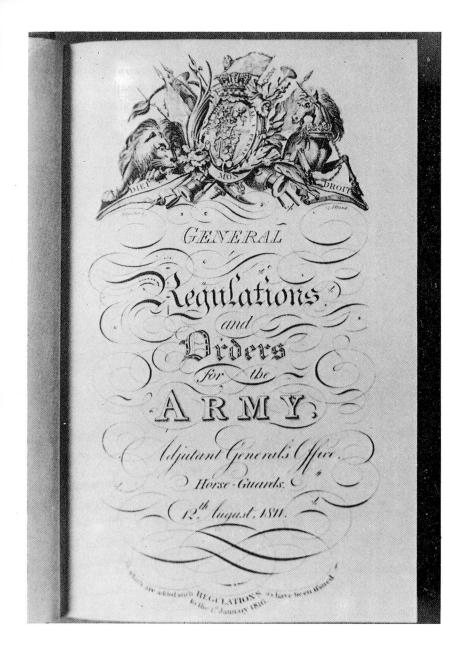

considered with good reason to be virtually unbeatable.

Still, problems were on the horizon, particularly in the colonies.

Years of war had taken their toll of available young men. Threats of invasion had caused the raising of fencible and local militia regiments and men enlisted in them were men lost to the serving Regular Army. Recruiting, then, became a contest of wills and wits. Men were lured into the Regular Army by promises of quick promotion, plentiful food and the chance of rich loot, as well as that old standby – alcohol.

Officers bought their way into their posts. Regulations required a minimum age of sixteen, and a recommendation outlining the prospective officer's 'character, Education and Bodily Health, and that he is prepared immediately to join any Regiment to which he may be appointed. His Christian Name and Place of Address must also be particularly stated.'

Commissions were expensive. The starting-place, the rank of ensign in any of the Regular regiments of foot, cost £400 – officially, with a little more money generally being required to pass under the table. A cornet of dragoons was required to part with £735. And for anyone who wished to hold the high rank of lieutenant-colonel of Foot Guards, the starting-price was £6,700. One could, and many did, pass up through the ranks by ability and luck, but purchase was the surest and most common method of promotion.

Needless to say, this system assured that men of property, tied to the status quo, became leaders in the army. They need not necessarily have been the best, brightest or most suited for the job: it is surprising how often they were.

Commissions were not purchased in the Royal Artillery and Royal Engineers. Most of their officers were the intelligent sons of middle-class families and received mathematical and scientific educations at the Royal Military Academy in Woolwich. Officers of those corps were not responsible to the army's Commander-in-Chief, but to the Board of Ordnance, and were promoted strictly according to seniority and merit.

Once men were enlisted, they had to be housed and fed. A sergeant of the 43rd Foot, not long before that regiment was sent to America, recalled that after his enlistment he found that, 'The sleeping room of which I was an inmate was an oblong building of unusually large dimensions, and was occupied by three companies, of an hundred men each. They were chiefly volunteers, and, of course, young soldiers, many were Irish, many more were English, several Welshmen were intermingled, and a few Scotch men came in to complete the whole. Most of these, and that was the only point of general resemblance, had indulged in excessive drinking. Some were uproariously merry, on others the effect was directly the reverse; and nothing less than a fight, it matter not with whom, would satisfy. Meantime, as they were unable to abuse each other in language mutually intelligible, exclamations profoundly jocular or absurdly rancorous ran through the building. . . . In a few weeks we marched to more convenient quarters, a few miles distance. The salutary restraints of discreetly managed discipline spoke chaos with order, and my situation became comparatively comfortable.'

Besides excessive drink, which was not issued, the British soldier was to receive a six-pound loaf of bread every four days, for which he was charged fivepence, and three-quarters of a pound daily of 'good, sound, sweet, and wholesome Meat (either Ox or Heifer Beef, or Wether or Ewe Mutton)' for which he paid sixpence a pound.

The soldier had to be uniformed, as well. The private of a Regular regiment of foot received a felt shako, eight inches tall, called a 'stovepipe'. It had an ornate brass plate in front with a cockade and regimental button over the plate. Over the cockade was a woollen tuft, white for

The 'stove-pipe' shako-plate, left, and the 'Belgic' shako-plate. (Drawings by Rebecca Katcher)

Buttons of the 8th (King's) Regiment of Foot, 10th Royal Veteran Battalion, 21st, 102nd and 104th Regiments of Foot. (Drawings by Rebecca Katcher)

grenadiers, green for light infantry and red and white for battalion men – there being one grenadier, one light and eight battalion companies per battalion.

In 1811 the Duke of Wellington ordered a new cap, copied from the Portuguese, which had a simpler brass plate; the tuft was now on the side, there were decorative white cords, and a false front gave added height. Except for troops in the New Orleans campaign, who had served on the Peninsula, troops in America seemed to have worn the 'stovepipe' shako exclusively.

The wool uniform coatee was cut quite tight, with a collar reaching to the chin, and short tails. Of scarlet for sergeants and officers and brick red for other ranks, it had a collar, cuffs and shoulder-straps of different colours for the different regiments. At the end of each shoulder-strap was a coarse, fringed tuft of wool. Across the chest, either evenly or in pairs, was sewn worsted white tape with different colours for different regiments woven in. Pewter buttons had regimental numbers and designs on them; officers' buttons were similar but of gold or silver.

Non-commissioned ranks wore their rank badges on the upper right arm of their sleeves. After the plain sleeves of the privates, came the one chevron, point down, of regimental lace worn by 'chosen men'. Corporals had two chevrons of regimental lace. Sergeants, in addition to their three chevrons, wore scarlet wool worsted sashes with a stripe of facing colour in the centre, and carried brass-hilted swords. Flank company and light infantry sergeants carried fusils, while others had pikes.

Sergeants wore three plain white chevrons, as well as plain white lace on their coats. Colour sergeants wore one chevron of plain lace with a Union flag and crossed swords in full colour above it. Sergeants-major wore four silver chevrons.

Sergeants and flank company sergeants-major wore chevrons on both arms, while flank company colour-sergeants wore the Union flag on their right arms, and chevrons on their left. All chevrons were sewn on pieces of facing colour cloth.

Officers wore crimson silk sashes. Officers of the 93rd (Highlanders) wore two epalettes. Company officers of the light infantry regiments, the 43rd, 60th and 93rd, wore a wing on each shoulder with a grenade or bugle on the strap, as did flank company officers in Regular regiments.

Regular regimental company officers wore one epaulette on the right shoulder. The major had two, each with a star on it. The lieutenant-colonel's pair had crowns on them, and the colonel's both a crown and a star.

When not on duty men of some regiments could wear plain white wool jackets, with cuffs, collars and shoulder-straps of facing colours. A small wool cap, like the First World War German *mütze*, completed the picture. The cap usually was made from an old coat, with a stripe of facing colour around the band and often with a pompon.

Trousers were of dark blue-grey wool, although in Canada they were often made from local materials and varied considerably. Dark grey gaiters were worn underneath.

Boots, or shoes, varied too. Something called 'beef boots', which appear to be ankle-length boots, were issued in Canada. A private of the 95th at this time wrote: 'I got a pair of boots, put them on, and threw my old ones away; but before I had walked four miles further my other boot bottom dropped off, and I had to walk barefooted, as my stocking feet were soon cut all to pieces. I was not alone in this predicament; many of the men were served the same. These boots were manufactured in England, and we said the soles and heels had been glued or pegged on, as there could not have been any wax or hemp used.

'I had worn out my shirts; the one I had on did not reach to my waist. I found a sheet in a house from which its occupants had fled; and a tailor in the regiment had cut me a shirt out of it; so here I resolved to finish it if possible. I did it, and put it on.'

Basic accoutrements consisted of a black cartridge box holding sixty rounds, suspended from a whitened buff leather sling with two brass buckles, and a whitened buff belt holding the bayonet scabbard with a metal regimental belt-plate in front.

In addition, the soldier carried a white duck haversack, closed with two plain pewter buttons, in which he carried his rations, and a blue-painted waterbottle suspended from a brown buckled leather belt. The waterbottle was usually marked with a broad white arrow and regimental number.

A black-painted knapsack, held up with white buff straps and braced with a frame inside, carried all his spare clothing, while the grey blanket was rolled and buckled on top.

On a short movement, as at North Point, Lieutenant George Grieg, 85th Foot, reported they carried three days' provisions, as well as 'A blanket, with a spare shirt and pair of shoes, was considered enough for each man . . . while brushes and other articles of that description were divided between comrades, one carrying what would suffice for both. Thus the additional load of twenty cartridges was more than counterbalanced by the clothing and necessities left behind.' Grieg pointed out the private's typical load was, '. . . arms and sixty rounds of ball cartridge . . . a knapsack containing shirts, shoes, stockings, etc., a blanket a haversack with provisions for three days, and a canteen or wooden keg filled with water.'

Uniform was a particular problem in Canada. Officers and men were used to the Duke of Wellington's army. Said one of his officers, 'Provided we brought our men into the field well appointed, and with sixty rounds of good ammunition each, he never looked to see whether their trousers were black, blue or grey, and as to ourselves [officers] we might be rigged out in all colours of the rainbow if we fancied it.'

Prevost was no Iron Duke, and he impressed his authority by having uniform regulations followed to the letter. On 23 August 1814 he issued an order: 'The Commander of the Forces has observed in the dress of Several of the Officers of Corps & Departments, lately added to this Army from that of Field Marshal the Duke of Wellington, a fancible vanity inconsistent with the rules of the Service, and in Some instances without Comfort or Convenience and to the prejudice of the Service, by removing essential distinctions of Rank and description of Service.

'His Excellency deems it expedient to direct that the General Officers in Charge of Divisions & Brigades do uphold His Majesty's Commands in that respect, and only admit of such deviations from them as may be justified by particular causes of Service and Climate – and even then uniformity is to be retained.

'Commanding Officers are held responsible that the Established Uniform of their Corps is strictly observed by the Officers under their Command.' Such an order did not add greatly to Sir George's respect from the Peninsular veterans.

The basic infantry weapon was a ·75-calibre, smoothbore India Pattern 'Brown Bess' flintlock musket. Capable of being fired almost four times a minute, the basic musket had been little changed over the past century. The barrel was held to the walnut stock by flat keys and three brass pipes held the ramrod under it. An iron eighteen-inch-long bayonet was attached to the browned barrel by a socket.

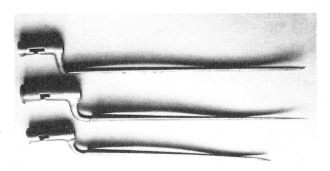

From top, a British fusil bayonet, a regular British 'Brown Bess' bayonet, and an American bayonet. (Author's collection)

The 43rd Foot, a light infantry regiment, had light model muskets with a thirty-nine-inch, unlike the regular forty-two-inch, barrel and a rear sight, which the other ones lacked.

While the 'Bess' served long and well, it was inferior in several ways to the American musket. It had a larger bore than the ·69 calibre American model, meaning the American weapon was lighter, and the American soldier's ammunition load was considerably lighter. In addition, the American system of barrel bands, instead of flat keys, made it easier to care for the weapon. The India Pattern's brass furniture was easier to care for than the American's rusting iron, however.

The 95th and some Canadian troops had Baker rifles. These had rifled barrels, sights, a patch box and a pistol grip for sharpshooting. The bayonet was a sword type with a brass grip. Accurate and deadly in the hands of men trained as were the 95th, the Baker was an excellent weapon. Again, however, it was somewhat inferior to the American issue rifle. As it fired a heavier ball, it was much heavier than the American model, while its barrel was shorter, giving the American riflemen an advantage in both weight and range.

Once uniformed and armed, the man was sent to join his regiment. Regiments in Canada had some unique problems. A regiment stationed there was generally divided into eight parts, many miles apart, where they stayed for some three years.

There the men were constantly tempted to desert by American agents, as well as seeing for themselves how people of no previous property or friends were making fortunes and becoming landed gentry. Desertion became almost the rule, and even the best of officers found that discipline was very difficult to maintain.

Officers in Canada were not necessarily the best, either, the most ambitious wanting to be with Wellington, and a Canadian wrote that, 'we got the rubbish of every department in the army. Any man whom the Duke deemed unfit for the Peninsula was considered quite good enough for the Canadian market.' Brock called the 41st Foot 'wretchedly officered'.

Then, too, only six wives per regiment were allowed. Stories of pregnant wives drawing the hated slip of paper, 'Not To Go', and their husbands sailing off never to see them again were legion, and they did not make for good morale.

In the 49th one officer's extreme severity resulted in an attempted mutiny, for which seven other ranks were executed.

Discipline, in any post, was very harsh. The lash was the mainstay of punishment, and 100 strokes were considered light punishment. Punishment parade was a formal affair, with all the men drawn up in a square looking inwards. The offender was tied to a triangle of halberds in the middle, while the commanding officer, medical officer and drum major looked on. Drummers did the actual flogging, relieving each other on every twenty-fifth stroke.

A civilian hoping to see the medical officer of the 4th Foot, shortly before it was sent to America, wrote: '. . . the 4th, or King's Own Regiment of Foot, [was] then lying in the same barracks. That regiment was then on parade, and it was a punishment parade – some sixteen poor fellows were waiting to receive their allowances, varying from 200 to 500 lashes.

'A gentleman standing near me, inquired the name or number of the regiment, and the answer he received was, that the men were called the King's Own, but he thought the officers must be the Devil's Own.'

Few, save some officers and senior sergeants, thought flogging did any good in maintaining discipline and on 25 March 1812 award of the lash by regimental courts-martial was limited and more than 300 lashes were prohibited.

Brock felt the answer to the problems in Canada was the posting of a Royal Veteran Battalion, which was then done in 1808. Such a battalion was made up of, '. . . *Meritorious* Soldiers, who by Wounds, Infirmity, or Age, are become unequal to the more active Duties of the Line, but who retain sufficient Strength for the less laborious Duties of a Garrison. . . .' Each man of the 10th was given 200 acres of land in Canada for enlisting.

Although more settled, spending time farming as well as soldiering, they still had many typical Regulars' faults. Roberts, Fort St Joseph's commander, said his men of the 10th were '. . . so debilitated and worn down by unconquerable drunkenness that neither the fear of punishment, the love of fame or the honour of country can animate them to extraordinary exertions.'

Despite these problems, the British Army was well trained and quite efficient in the field. They

1: Captain, 49th Regt., 1812
2: Gunner, Royal Regt. of Artillery, 1812
3: Corporal, Royal Newfoundland (Fencible) Regt., 1812

A

1: Private, 16th US Infantry Regt., 1812
2: Private, US 4th Rifle Regt., 1814
3: Musician, US Foot Artillery, 1812

B

1: Sergeant, 10th Royal Veterans Bn., 1812
2: Private, Royal Marines, 1812
3: Major-General, British Army, 1812

1: Sergeant, US Light Artillery, 1812
2: Sergeant, 22nd US Infantry Regt., 1813
3: Corporal, Pioneers, 25th Inf. Regt., 1814

D

1: Chosen Man, Upper Canada Militia, 1813
2: Major, lower Canada Militia Bn., 1813
3: Musician, Canadian Fencibles, 1814

E

1: Private, Rifle Co., Michigan Legionary Corps, 1812
2: Lieutenant, Baltimore United Volunteers, 1814
3: Major-General, US Army, 1813

F

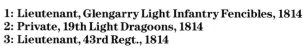

1: Lieutenant, Glengarry Light Infantry Fencibles, 1814
2: Private, 19th Light Dragoons, 1814
3: Lieutenant, 43rd Regt., 1814

2

1

3

G

1: Private, 5th US Infantry Regt., 1815
2: Private, US Light Dragoons, 1814
3: Master Workman, US Corps of Artificers, 1814

H

had learned well the lessons of the Peninsular campaign. They generally picked defensive positions, as Grieg reported, '. . . immediately under the ridge . . . in order to prevent their disposition from being seen by the enemy should they come to attack.'

On the march, as on the way to Bladensburg, they sent out three separate advance guards· to prevent surprise, as well as parties of forty to fifty men as flank guards, sweeping the woods and fields to a distance of nearly half a mile. The army halted when it reached a defensible location, even if it had only marched eight miles that day.

When attacked they generally followed Wellingtonian practice and fired in two ranks. An eyewitness at New Orleans, however, saw that they '. . . still kept up the old custom of firing three deep; one row of men half-kneeling, and the other two ranks firing over their shoulders. This style of firing, along with the darkness of the evening, explained to me the reason of why the enemy's balls, which we heard whistling by, mostly flew over our heads.'

Generally, however, British fire power was sufficient to sweep any field, and it would be followed up by a final bayonet charge.

Left, a private's sword of the Royal Artillery, right a 1796-pattern foot officer's sword with its original scarlet and gold sword knot. (Author's collection)

25

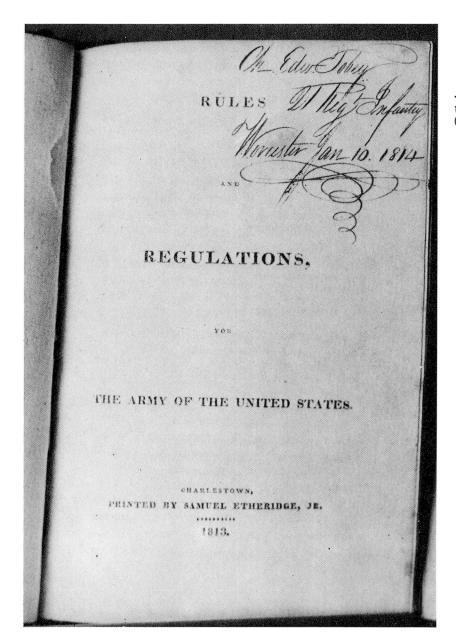

The American Army

As a republic which had not too long before defeated a major standing army in a revolution, one cause of which was that standing army itself, the United States did not have much of a Regular, or standing, Army at the war's outbreak.

In 1808 Congress had authorized a Regular Army of 175 officers and 2,389 enlisted men. These men were to be enlisted with a bounty of $16 and receive on their discharge five years later, 160 acres of land and three months' pay. A private's pay was $5 a month and, in a developing country like the United States in 1812 where the average day labourer could earn at least $9 a month, very few people were interested in a military career.

Enlisted men, therefore, were often deserters from the British Army in Canada or men on the run from the law somewhere.

In 1802 the United States Military Academy, at West Point, New York, was officially founded. Until the war actually broke out, however, the U.S.M.A. was not developed into a real, worthwhile school, and most officers were trained by serving with regiments in the field. Their training was, therefore, more of the practical school of experience, than theoretical.

The army's 'rules with regard to promotion', called for 'original vacancies' to be filled by selection, while 'accidental vacancies' were made by seniority. Furthermore, 'Promotions to the rank of captain, will be made *regimentally*; to that of field appointments, by *line*, the light artillery, dragoons, artillery, infantry, and riflemen, being kept always distinct.'

Although promotions were given by seniority and/or ability, the policies of Congress which had constantly enlarged and reduced the army's size had created a feeling among its most capable officers that there was no future in its ranks. Many of the more able men had gone into private life. Those remaining were apt to be unlearned and, at best, indifferent officers. In 1811, for example, the Captain commanding Fort Knox fled the territory after shooting and killing a subordinate officer.

When the army was enlarged in 1808 a number of new officers were appointed, again without much specialised military training. Among them were Zachary Taylor and Winfield Scott, both of whom were to gain fame later. Scott considered his fellow appointees 'coarse and ignorant', 'decayed gentlemen', and 'imbeciles and ignoramuses'.

In January 1812, when war seemed likely, Congress authorized a Regular Army of 35,603. There were actually no more than 4,000 serving at the time. In February, one year enlistments for 30,000 volunteers were allowed. By May the army had grown to 6,744.

Among the troops authorized were six companies of United States Rangers, five of which were actually raised in Ohio, Indiana, Illinois and Kentucky.

In April 15,000 eighteen-month additional enlistments were planned and, with the coming of war, men began to join up more rapidly. Never, however, was it easy to fill the Regular ranks. According to the adjutant-general, '. ... although the numerical force in January, 1814, was 23,614, the actual strength of the army at that time was less than half that number, arising from the expiration of the term of service of the troops raised in 1809 and enlisted for five years, and of the twelve and eighteen-months troops enlisted in 1812–1813.' Congress had previously raised a private's pay to $10 a month, and now awarded enlistment bounties of $124, and 320 acres of land on discharge.

Congress also divided the country into nine – later ten – military districts and assigned different regiments to recruit out in each one. Two companies of light artillery, three troops of the 2nd Light Dragoons, one battalion of the 1st Artillery, and the 4th, 9th and 21st Infantry Regiments would recruit in Massachusetts and New Hampshire. Rhode Island and Connecticut would provide men for one troop of the 2nd Light Dragoons, one battalion of the 1st Artillery and the 25th Infantry. Two companies of light artillery, two troops of the 2nd Light Dragoons, two battalions of the 3rd Artillery and the 6th and 15th Infantry were to come from parts of New York and New Jersey. The rest of New Jersey, Pennsylvania and Delaware would supply men for two companies of light artillery, two troops of the 2nd Light Dragoons, a battalion of the 2nd Artillery, the 3rd, 5th, 16th and 22nd Infantry. Two companies of light artillery, a troop of the 1st Light Dragoons, one and a half battalion

Buttons of the 3rd Artillery, 1st Rifle Regiments, the general issue button, the 1st Light Artillery and the 9th Infantry Regiments. (Drawings by Rebecca Katcher)

The coat worn by John Wool when a captain in the 13th Infantry in 1813. (Courtesy Rensselaer County Historical Society)

Back view of Captain Wool's coat. (Courtesy Rensselaer County Historical Society)

of the 2nd Artillery, the 12th, 14th and 20th Infantry would be drawn from Maryland and Virginia.

Further south, both Carolinas and Georgia were to send men into two troops of the 1st Light Dragoons, a battalion of the 1st Artillery, the 8th, 10th and 18th Infantry. Two troops of the 1st Light Dragoons, a battalion of the 1st Artillery, the 2nd, 7th and 24th Infantry, and three companies of riflemen would be drawn from Louisiana, the Mississippi territory and Tennessee.

Out west, Kentucky, Ohio, the Indiana territory, Michigan, Illinois and Missouri were to send men into two companies of light artillery, three troops of the 1st Light Dragoons, one and a half battalions of the 2nd Artillery, the 1st, 17th, 19th Infantry, and four rifle companies. Two troops of the 2nd Light Dragoons, two battalions

of the 3rd Artillery, the 11th, 13th and 23rd Infantry and three rifle companies were to come from northern New York and Vermont.

Other regiments were recruited where needed.

The uniform the army first went to war in was an elaborate one. The felt shako was between $6\frac{7}{8}$ and $7\frac{1}{4}$ inches tall, with a $2\frac{1}{2}$ inch visor, and cords and tassels and a front plate, '. . . with the eagle, the number of the regiment and designation of the service.' The coatee, with short tails, was of dark blue with red cuffs and collar, reaching to the earlobe. The coat was laced with white worsted tape across the chest, on the cuffs and on the collar. Pants were gaitered trousers, or overalls, supposedly grey but also seen in brown and green. Officers' trousers were blue wool and generally tucked into boots.

Non-commissioned officers wore the same coat

28

as privates. Corporals wore one white wool worsted fringed epaulette on the right shoulder. Sergeants – unlike the British Army, the American Army had only one rank of sergeant – had two white epaulettes. In addition, sergeants wore a scarlet wool worsted sash and carried an iron-hilted straight sword. Artillery non-commissioned officers dressed the same, only with yellow epaulettes and brass-hilted swords.

Officers wore similar plain coats, with only the red collar being set off by silver lace. They carried brass-hilted swords and wore crimson silk sashes. A subaltern wore a silver epaulette on his left shoulder; a captain, the same on the right shoulder; and field officers, on both shoulders. Officers made minor changes in the uniform to suit themselves, and often wore fancier-than-issue swords and cap-plates.

An infantry soldier carried on his right hip, suspended from a whitened buff leather belt, a black leather cartridge box, '. . . with blocks bored for 26 cartridges of ball nineteen to the pound of stout leather, having under the block a tin container of three compartments for 6 cartridges to be in each end compartment and for flints and oil rags in the middle one. To this a little leather

The epaulette of Ensign John Reese, 5th Maryland Infantry Regiment, worn at the Battle of North Point. (Fort McHenry National Monument and Historic Shrine)

A wood canteen painted black with a red 'U.S.' Sky blue was a more common overall colour. (Smithsonian Institution)

U.S. 1813 leather shako, with an infantry plate, showing the rain flap worn down. (Author's collection)

pocket in front of the box affords admittance.'

On his left side hung his bayonet scabbard on a whitened buff belt with a plain pewter oval belt-plate in front. The iron bayonet had a sixteen-inch-long, triangular-shaped blade.

Over that hung a linen haversack, generally waterproofed by painting, and a light blue painted wooden canteen. Usually his regimental designation was painted on that in red or white.

His knapsack was also painted blue, usually with a large red 'U.S.' in the centre, and he carried his grey blanket and greatcoat folded inside it.

It became impossible to provide the nicely designed coatees in a country as little industrial-ized as the United States, especially after the British naval blockade. In 1813 a new uniform was substituted. It consisted of, 'A plain blue coatee, without a particle of red to it, with white or buff cross belts, white vests & white overalls with black gaiters for Infantry & Artillery.... The coats should be 'single breasted, to button from the collar to the waist.' White lace was left only to decorate the collar.

In 1813, as well, a new shako, copied from the British Belgic shako, was adopted. It was made of leather, instead of felt, because leather, '... will last three to four years with decency, under any circumstances two years, [while] the latter [of felt] but one year and will not look decent half that time, the first wetting injures its good appearance. . . .' The new shako had its plume on the left and cord from the bottom of the left to the top of the right, with two tassels thereon. A separate piece of thin leather was sewn in the back, to be used for protection in the rain. The overall height was about the same as before.

Actually, even this simpler and more serviceable uniform became impossible to supply regularly. In the winter of 1812 clothing ordered in September for the 17th, 19th and 24th Infantry did not arrive and local women made up 1,800 heavy shirts for them. Even shoes were lacking and only in December were they available.

On the Niagara frontier General Scott required uniforms for his brigade and was told by the Quartermaster in Philadelphia that it was impossible to obtain blue wool. Would Scott mind if his men wore plain grey coats? Scott was more worried about training his men than dressing them and took the coats – much to the men's disgust, grey wool being generally reserved for common labourers and slaves.

In a country as large, with as many different climates as the United States, light-weight, summer uniforms were needed as well as woollen ones. South of the Potomac River, therefore, white linen coatees, with long sleeves but no tails, and with nine small buttons, were issued. With the large numbers enlisted in 1812, it was necessary to issue them in the north, too, but by 1814 they were once again limited to the south. In summer in the north, grey sleeved waistcoats were worn.

The American musket, made in Springfield, Harper's Ferry or by contractors, was a copy of the 1777 French musket, with all iron furniture and a ·69-calibre bore. Cadets at the U.S.M.A. received special, light-weight models of this type. Riflemen received a half-stocked rifle, firing a 54-calibre ball, with a brass patch box.

The uniformed, armed soldier generally found himself stationed in a fort, perhaps on the frontier fighting Indians, or near a large city as part of its defence.

The typical fort may well be Fort McHenry, near Baltimore. Located some distance from town, sixty officers and men made up its garrison. Every twenty enlisted men lived in a single barrack-room, with a single fireplace and wood bunks with straw mattresses which slept four and sometimes six men each. Other furniture included tables, chairs and benches, for it was in the barrack-room that the men were to spend their spare time. Junior officers got a room each, while the commander and adjutant shared four rooms. Officers' families generally came with them, but enlisted men were discouraged from marrying.

Men in linen U.S. Regular summer uniforms stand behind the fortifications at New Orleans where Andrew Jackson's men held off the British attack. (Courtesy Melville Cohen IV)

31

Officers lived in the first floor of the right-hand building, while enlisted men lived in all the other barracks. The three cannon now sit on the parade ground of Fort McHenry.

Two hours a day on six days a week were devoted to drill in full uniform. The drill had been the Revolutionary War's Baron von Steuben's version of Prussian drill, but, in 1812, gave way to Colonel Alexander Smyth and Lieutenant-Colonel William Duane's version of French drill.

On Sunday mornings there was a full inspection, following a Saturday night cleaning of the barrack-rooms, weapons and uniforms.

Other than that, sentry duty was the major event of the soldier's life. Sentries had to see that no civilians got into the fort, or soldiers without leave got out. At times they had to check men leaving the fort to see they weren't sneaking out rations or clothes to sell or trade for drinks. After the recapture of Fort Detroit, the fort's commanding officer constantly had to give orders against soldiers selling their clothing or increasing the provision problems by distilling grain.

One man from each company was named company gardener, and took charge of the company's plot in the fort's vegetable garden. Other men drew police duty, picking up rubbish, sweeping out the barracks, airing blankets and

doing light labour. Each company was allowed to employ four laundresses, sometimes soldiers' wives, who did much of this cleaning.

In a frontier, growing country, the army represented a labour resource for doing things like building roads. If a labour party worked on this non-military type of project for over ten days, it became 'fatigue duties', and the men received an extra ten cents daily and an extra gill of liquor. Even with the extras, fatigues were disliked.

A man didn't really need another gill of liquor as he already received one gill of rum, whisky or brandy daily (officers, but not the men, were allowed to take twenty cents per gill instead of the ration). He also received daily $1\frac{1}{4}$ lb. of beef or $\frac{3}{4}$ lb. of pork, 18 oz. of bread or flour, and lesser amounts of salt, vinegar, soap and candles. The whole ration cost the government fifteen cents.

Other little luxuries, such as tobacco or beer, could be purchased at the sutlers'. Each post had one sutler and the men were allowed to go in debt one-third of a month's pay at the sutler's – leading to constant debt.

Constant debt led to disciplinary problems, and

the most common were drunkenness, disobedience to orders, desertion and stealing. Flogging had been originally allowed in the American Army, although seventy-five was about the maximum lashes given. In 1812 Congress outlawed, '... the infliction of corporeal punishment by stripes or lashes.' Old habits die hard, and men were still sometimes flogged with a 'colt', a short rope with a knotted end. Shortly after the new law a corporal beat a private for getting in his way. The soldier then brought charges against the corporal. The private himself then was charged with, '... unsoldierly conduct & using disrespectful & insolent language.' He was found guilty, but the court thought he had already suffered enough at the corporal's hands and no punishment was awarded.

More commonly, two privates who disobeyed orders ended up in the guardhouse for a month, forfeited half that month's pay, and had a ball and chain attached to one of their legs during their imprisonment.

Non-commissioned officers were generally stripped of rank before the entire regiment or company on parade.

Desertion was probably the most serious offence. Deserters were sought by advertisements in newspapers, as this one in the *Vermont Sentinel*: 'Ten dollars reward for John Fisk, an enlisted soldier from the barracks at Burlington, offered by Richard Bean, Lieutenant, 11th Regiment, U.S. Infantry.' A typical punishment for desertion would be for the deserter to spend the rest of his enlistment at hard labour and pay the costs involved in his apprehension by having half his monthly pay withheld for a year.

It's one thing to recruit, dress, arm and house a group of men. It's quite another to convert that group to an army capable of winning battles.

An inspecting officer's report on the 14th Infantry in 1812, soon to lose their regimental colours to the 49th Foot, probably summed up the whole American Army so quickly called up. 'The 14th is composed entirely of recruits; they appear to be almost as ignorant of their duty as if they had never seen a camp, and scarcely know on which shoulder to carry the musket. They are mere militia, and, if possible, even worse; and if taken into action in their present state, will prove

more dangerous to themselves than to their enemy.'

The officer corps, damaged by earlier Congressional whims and made up often of inexperienced men, was most to blame. It was, therefore, that the Baltimore newspaper *Nile's Weekly Register* reported to its readers, 'with great pleasure', on 14 August 1813, that, 'gen. Hampton is busily employed in making *soldiers* of the *officers* of the army at *Burlington*. They are frequently and severely drilled; and given to understand that they *must* and *shall* ascertain and perform their several duties. This is striking at the very root of our disasters. The best materials for an army that the world could furnish, have been sacrificed to the pompous ignorance or inconsiderable courage of those who should have applied them to victory.'

Once officers had learned their duties, men could, too, and Major Jesup, commanding the

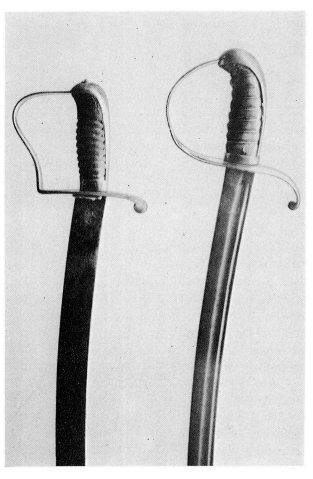

American cavalry sabres. (Smithsonian Institution)

A leather cockade with brass eagle worn on an officer's *chapeau-de-bras*. (Smithsonian Institution)

American artillery officer's sword and scabbard. (Smithsonian Institution)

25th Infantry, wrote that, ' . . . he began, under the orders of General Scott, a course of instruction, and kept his command under arms from seven to ten hours a day. A similar course was pursued by the chiefs of other corps. The consequence was, that when we took the field in July our corps manœuvred in action and under the fire of the enemy's artillery with the accuracy of parade.'

Once under fire, a well-trained and equipped army could hold its own against the best of Wellington's veterans. Instructions of how to win were quite explicit. On 27 November 1812, General Smyth wrote to Lieutenant-Colonel Winder, 14th Infantry, giving instructions for battle tactics: '1. The artillery will spend some of their first shot on the enemy's artillery, and then aim at the infantry, raking them where it is practicable. 2. The firing of musketry by wings or companies will begin at the distance of two hundred yards, aiming at the middle and firing deliberately. 3. At twenty yards' distance the soldiers will be ordered to trail arms, advance with shouts, fire at five paces' distance and charge bayonets. 4. The soldiers will be silent, above all things, attentive at the word of command, load quick and well and aim low.'

Despite training or instructions like these, there was a healthy feeling of respect for the red-coated veterans of so many battles fought against the best troops the conqueror of Europe could throw against them. At the night battle outside New Orleans Lieutenant-Colonel Ross, commanding the 7th and 44th Infantry, held them back from hand-to-hand contact with the British, feeling his men would have little chance crossing cold steel with British Regulars.

Regardless of this feeling, which was far from universal, by the last years of the war the American Army had been moulded to a hard-fighting, well-equipped, well-led little band capable of taking on the best Britain had to offer.

The Militia

Both the United States and Canada set up rather similar militia organizations. In both cases each community had a standing militia of all able-bodied men, between the ages of sixteen and sixty, each of whom was to own his own musket and was required to serve in one or two annual musters. Such militia organizations were lax in discipline, training and uniform. Both countries, therefore, set up, as well as the ordinary militia, other types of units.

In the United States these took the form of local volunteer companies. They bore such splendid names as the four companies which defended St Michael on 10 August 1813: the Easton Fencibles, Mechanic Volunteers, Hearts of Oak, and Independent Volunteers. Splendidly clad in uniforms they themselves designed and provided, they drilled usually weekly, and made up the heart of any local defence.

Even with the fancy dress and more frequent meetings, the volunteer companies were no match for Regulars. They may have called themselves light infantry, but as District of Columbia Militia Brigade-Major John S. Williams wrote:

The design of a painted militia knapsack. (Smithsonian Institution)

'. . . as a cowl does not make a monk, to dress and equip a body of men as light infantry or dragoons does not make them what they are called. They must be disciplined and have some experience in the peculiar duties, before they are entitled to the name.

'A company of cavalry, formed in the heart of a large commercial city, might choose to assume the name of "Cossacks" and provide themselves with lances and other suitable equipments, but they would remain, in reality, just what they were before – a parcel of inoffensive clerks or journeymen mechanics.'

When the enemy – American or British – threatened, however, everyone was needed. Such was the case in August 1814, when Captain James H. Rogers sent out the following typical order to his company of the 51st Maryland Militia Regiment: 'Sir, In obedience to a Regimental Order, you will furnish yourself with a Knapsack, Canteen and Ten rounds ball Cartridges, suitable to your Firelock, and hold yourself in readiness to repair immediately to my quarters on the George Town Road, with arms and accoutrements, upon any Alarm that may be given, by the ringing of the watch bell. Our Enemy is at the door, therefore it is hoped that no Man, who wishes well to his Country, will be missing.'

When the alarm bell did ring, Canadians came out either in civilian dress or in uniforms patterned closely in cut and colour after British ones. American dress varied tremendously according to area and type of unit. The mounted Tennesseans at New Orleans were noted by an eyewitness 'In their woollen hunting shirts and copperas dyed pantaloons; with slouched hats made from the skins of racoons or foxes; with belts of untanned deer-skin in which were stuck their hunting knives and tomahawks – with their long unkempt hair and unshorn faces. . . .'

On the other hand, a private of the 5th Maryland Militia Regiment wore to the Battle of Bladensburg a '. . . winter cloth uniform, with a most absurd helmet of thicked jacked leather and covered with plumes. We carried, besides, a knapsack in which – in my own case – I had packed the greatcoat, my . . . blanket, two or three shirts, stockings, etc. Among these articles I had also put a pair of pumps which I had provided with the idea that, after we had beaten the British army and saved Washington, Mr. Madison would very likely invite us to a ball at the President's House, and I wanted to be ready for it.'

A majority of Lower Canadians were French, and those not in the Select Embodied Militia, kept their native dress. A British doctor, bound for his regiment, met a company of them wearing, '. . . capots and trowsers of home-spun stuff, and their blue tunques (a cap like a nightcap) were all of the same cut and colour, which gave them an air of uniformity that added much to their military look. . . .'

In Upper Canada units called 'incorporated' and 'Provincial' corps were recruited, dressed, trained and served full-time, as Regular regiments. In 1813, for example, the Volunteer Incorporated Militia, wearing red coats with dark green facings and the rest of the Regular uniform was raised for full-time service during the war.

Lower Canada, of whose 60,000 militia only some 2,000 had received any type of training, raised six battalions of Select Embodied Militia.

Brass belt-plate of the 1st Battalion of Select Embodied Militia. (Drawing by Rebecca Katcher)

Although some elements were at a few actions, they generally did garrison duty, freeing the Regulars for more aggressive duty.

Despite uniforms and arms, or the lack of them, the record of the militia on both sides was a mixed one. Prevost wrote that he felt it was unadvisable to arm the majority of Upper Canada militiamen, while Brock reported that, '. . . the disposition of the people is bad.' On the American side, a

Regular officer reported seeing some Ohio militiamen riding one of their officers out of camp on a rail, and General Hull told the commander of the 4th Infantry, 'Your regiment is a powerful argument. Without them I could not march these men to Detroit.'

Militiamen on both sides did come through, at places like Châteauguay, for the Canadians, and New Orleans for the Americans. For the most part Regulars made up the backbone of both sides' military efforts.

The Plates

A1: Captain, 49th Regiment of Foot, 1812
The 49th was one of a handful of Regular Army regiments in Canada in 1812. Other regiments included the 8th (dark blue facings/gold metal), 41st (red facings/silver metal), 98th (yellow facings/silver metal), 99th (yellow facings/silver metal), and 100th (yellow facings/silver metal).

A2: Gunner, Royal Regiment of Artillery, 1812
The gunner's two vent picks are worn on the centre of the gunner's pouch, while the red string suspends a small priming horn which hung over the pouch flap. The cord tied around either end of the horn and ended in large tassels.

A3: Corporal, Royal Newfoundland (Fencible) Regiment of Foot, 1812
Because of manpower pressures of the Napoleonic Wars, Canadian regiments, such as the Royal Newfoundland, were raised and equipped the same as their British counterparts. The wings and white shako tuft mark this corporal as being in the regimental grenadier company, hence chevrons on both arms.

B1: Private, 16th US Infantry Regiment, 1812
The 16th was organized 11 January 1812 in Philadelphia, Pennsylvania, and served at the captures of York and Fort George and the Battle of Crysler's Farm. The regiment received black instead of the regulation dark blue coatees, due to typical American supply problems, as its initial issue. Other regiments without blue coats were the 8th (black and brown coats), 10th (blue and brown), 12th (drab), 14th (drab and brown), 15th (grey or mixed), 17th (blue, brown, drab, and black), and 20th (drab and brown). Trousers came in a variety of colours, including green, brown, and grey.

B2: Private, US 4th Rifle Regiment, 1814
Green trimmed with yellow were the official rifle colours, but apparently only the 1st Rifle Regiment retained these colours for coatee and trousers use since the government could not find enough green cloth for a full supply. During the summer, however, riflemen preferred linen hunting shirts, as worn during the War of American Independence. These were made in rifle colours, although the winter coatees were grey with black trim for officers and men. The 4th was raised in Philadelphia in 1814.

B3: Musician, US Foot Artillery, 1812
Musicians, drummers and fifers in the US Army wore 'reverse clothing', i.e., their basic coat and facing colours were the opposite as worn by fighting men in their regiments. The regiments of foot artillery officially manned garrison guns, but many foot artillerymen saw infantry duty on the Canadian border.

C1: Sergeant, 10th Royal Veterans Battalion, 1812
The 10th was formed in Canada just before the war as a place to use men too old or infirm to fight. The battalion first received these gaiters and trousers and, although ordered into grey trousers in 1811, were allowed to wear them until worn out. This sergeant differs from most British Army sergeants, who carried swords and pikes, by his more practical, for the frontier, use of a musket.

C2: Private, Royal Marines, 1812
Royal Marines served not only in the many naval actions of the war, but two Royal Marine battalions were sent to Canada in the autumn of 1813 where they saw a great deal of action along the border. A third battalion was sent to Virginia in 1814, while other Royal Marines raided along the Georgia Coast, served in the New Orleans Campaign, and fought alongside the Creek and Choctaw Indians in Louisiana.

C3: Major-General, British Army, 1812
While a fancy, embroidered coat was worn for dress, this plainer version was preferred for field use. A major-general wore his buttons in pairs, with five pairs on each lapel, two above each cuff, and two on the waist at the coat's rear.

D1: Sergeant, The US Regiment of Light Artillery, 1812
Although the Regiment of Light Artillery, to include ten companies, had been authorized in 1808, only one company had been equipped as field artillery by 1812. When the war began, the Army recruited some horse (with every man mounted) and some field (some men walked) artillery companies. Both types served in the field rather than in fortifications.

D2: Sergeant, 22nd US Infantry Regiment, 1813
The 22nd, recruited in Pennsylvania in 1812, was typical in that the regulation uniform was unavailable for its recruits. Officers, who supplied their own uniforms, would have worn the regulation dark blue with red facings and silver lace. The 22nd also did not receive cap plates, which were in short supply, or buff equipment belts. The regiment served along the Niagara frontier.

D3: Corporal, Pioneers, 25th Infantry Regiment, 1814
The 25th, one of Winfield Scott's Brigade units, was one of the first in the US Army to organize pioneers. Ten men, one from each company, with a corporal commanding, formed the regimental pioneer squad. Each man wore a linen apron. Four pioneers were equipped with a felling axe and spade; two with a spade and pick axe; and four 'necessary tools in due proportions'. Scott's Brigade wore grey kersey roundabout jackets but did receive the new 1813 model leather shakos.

E1: Chosen Man, Upper Canada Militia, 1813
On 1 January 1813 this uniform was made regulation for Upper Canada's militia units, although often civilian clothing, with a white cotton brassard, served in emergencies. In May 1814 the militia received both green coats faced with yellow and red coats faced with dark and light green. On 21 June 1814 all officers were ordered to wear scarlet jackets with dark blue facings, gold buttons and lace around the cuffs and collar.

E2: Major, 1st Lower Canada Select Embodied Militia Battalion, 1813
Lower Canada had six Select Embodied Militia Battalions. The 1st always managed, apparently, to find red coatees, but the other battalions wore olive green jackets in early 1813. Red coatees issued in the summer of 1813 had the following facings: 1st, blue; 2nd, light green; 3rd, yellow; 4th, dark green; and 5th & 6th, black. Issues made in March 1814 changed the facings to: 1st, blue; 2nd, yellow; 3rd, green; and 4th, green.

E3: Musician, Canadian Fencibles, 1814
All but Royal Regiments of the British Army put their musicians into 'reverse clothing'. Elements of the Canadian Fencibles served at Chateauguay, Crysler's Farm, Salmon Falls, La Colle, and Plattsburg. The regiment garrisoned York and Fort George in 1815 before being demobilized in Quebec on 15 August 1815. Other Fencible regiments included the Nova Scotia Fencibles (yellow facings) and New Brunswick Fencibles (light yellow facings).

F1: Private, Rifle Company, Legionary Corps, Militia of the Territory of Michigan, 1812
Michigan's 'Legionary Corps' was formed in 1805 and was to contain cavalry (red coats faced black), artillery (blue coats faced red), light infantry (blue coats faced buff) and riflemen. The cavalry and riflemen served in the Detroit campaign, surrendering in 1812. Although the rifle company had had rifles when in Federal service in 1807, in 1812 the company apparently received smoothbore muskets.

F2: Lieutenant, Baltimore United Volunteers, 1814
This unit served during the British attack on Baltimore, as the 4th Company, 5th Regiment, Maryland Volunteer Infantry. The unit was so elegant that its privates all wore engraved sterling silver shoulder belt plates. The uniform, however, conforms to period regulation Maryland State dress rules.

F3: Major-General, US Army, 1813
Generals wore essentially the Army's staff uniform, save they could have embroidered buttonholes, although few did. The Commissary General of

Ordnance, Adjutants, Inspectors, Quartermasters General, and the Commissary General of Purchases were allowed embroidery only on collar buttonholes. Blue pantaloons were worn in winter. Yellow-hilted straight swords were worn by all but the Adjutant, Inspector, and Quartermaster Generals' officers, who wore sabres. Hospital Staff officers wore the same uniform save that they wore pocket flaps, black buttons, and four vertical black buttonholes on each cuff.

G1: Lieutenant, The Glengarry Light Infantry Fencible Regiment, 1814

The Glengarrys were raised in Upper Canada in 1812 largely from among Scottish veterans. Elements of the unit served at Ogdensburg, York, Fort George, Sacketts Harbor, Stoney Creek, Fort Oswego, Lundy's Lane, Fort Erie, and Cook's Mills. The dress was a copy of that worn by the 95th Rifles, although the men carried light infantry muskets and the unit had a colour.

G2: Private, 19th Regiment of Light Dragoons, 1814

Although there were a number of mounted Canadian units, the only British Army mounted unit to serve in North America during the war was the 19th. The unit arrived in Quebec on 17 May 1813 and served at Fort George, Black Rock, Buffalo, Queenston, Chippewa, Fort Erie, Long Point, and Lundy's Lane. The unit returned to the United Kingdom in 1816 and was disbanded in 1821.

G3 Lieutenant, 43rd Regiment of Foot, 1814

One of the Duke of Wellington's regiments sent to America, the 43rd, a light infantry regiment, saw service at New Orleans. The regiment wore the stovepipe shako, although other British foot units in the New Orleans campaign were probably the only ones in the war in America to wear the Belgic shakos made famous at Waterloo.

H1: Private, 5th US Infantry Regiment, 1815

In 1816 Charles Hamilton Smith, a British subject, drew several US soldiers while visiting the country. His are some of the few period drawings of the new uniform approved in 1813, which was to be plain blue with white lace trim. This figure is closely based on one of his sketches.

An **1813-pattern, leather, officer's shako with a non-regulation plate. (Smithsonian Institution)**

H2: Private, US Regiment of Light Dragoons, 1814

Although a number of volunteer militia mounted units served during the war, only two regular regiments of light dragoons were raised. They were largely wasted in scouting, courier, and escort work and the regiments were combined into one regiment in early 1814. On 3 March 1815 even this regiment was abolished as being too costly to maintain.

H3: Master Workman, US Corps of Artificers, 1814

The Corps, made up of masons, carpenters, blacksmiths, armourers, saddle and harness makers, ships' carpenters, boat builders, and labourers, was authorized in April 1812. It was mustered out on 3 March 1815. The unit was commanded by a superintendent, with assistants and master workmen under him who, in turn, supervised workmen and labourers. Yellow lace was worn by the latter two grades; the higher grades wore gold with red wings. The superintendent wore three stars on each wing; assistants, two; and master workmen, one.

INDEX

(References to illustrations are shown in **bold**. Plates are shown with caption locators in brackets.)